HEAT W

ALSO BY JULIAN STANNARD

Rina's War (Peterloo Poets, 2001)
The Red Zone (Peterloo Poets, 2007)
The Parrots of Villa Gruber Discover Lapis Lazuli (Salmon Poetry, 2011)
The Street of Perfect Love (Worple Press, 2014)
What were you thinking? (CB Editions, 2016)
Sottoripa: Genoese Poems (Canneto Editore, 2018)
Average is the New Fantastico (Green Bottle Press, 2019)

JULIAN STANNARD

Heat Wave

CROMER

PUBLISHED BY SALT PUBLISHING 2020

2 4 6 8 10 9 7 5 3 1

Copyright © Julian Stannard 2020

Julian Stannard has asserted his right under the Copyright, Designs
and Patents Act 1988 to be identified as the author of this work.

First published in Great Britain in 2020 by
Salt Publishing Ltd
12 Norwich Road, Cromer, Norfolk NR27 0AX United Kingdom

www.saltpublishing.com

Salt Publishing Limited Reg. No. 5293401

A CIP catalogue record for this book is available from the British Library

ISBN 978 1 78463 218 2 (Paperback edition)

Typeset in Sabon by Salt Publishing

For Jack and William

Contents

Lesson Plan

Walk with purpose into the room.
Bamboozle, baffle, kick-box.

Hand out Bulgarian poems.
Cite Spinoza. Invoke Foucault.

Retreat. Change city. Sleep a little.

Whoopsee

It was late Sunday evening
and I was on the Northern Line
and if the train was not exactly empty
there was enough floor space
for anyone who had a desire to move
their left leg out, their left leg in.

I seem to remember
Leonard Cohen's 'Dance with Me
to the End of Love' sobbed and

bobbed in my head.

I had a small suitcase on wheels
full of exam papers
which I had spent a week marking
with a strange intensity
as if I had taken that drug
which makes you concentrate
very hard and for hours at a stretch.

A small suitcase on wheels
full of exam papers
all marked and ready to go.

I was holding my suitcase
in the way you hold a dog,
quite gently, by its collar –
(there's a good dog, there's a good suitcase . . .)
but I must have taken my hand away.

It was then that the woman opposite me
shouted *Whoopsee!*

Who nowadays. I thought, goes
around shouting *Whoopsee?*

A middle-aged woman, a little crimped,
glasses and a milk-white coat,
a rather casual coat if you will.

Whoopsee!

And I turned to see the suitcase
on wheels moving at quite a pace
along the carriage of the train.

At first I started chasing it.
I had spent an entire week
working on those papers
but the train was
at quite a tilt

and the suitcase was
stretching its legs
imagining a moment
that the suitcase had legs.
I guess the wheels were its legs.

The suitcase was moving at such a pace
I just stood and watched it
as it passed into the next carriage
and continued its way not without grace
down the length of the train.

Occasionally I could hear
from afar, therefore slightly
muffled, some other weirdo

shouting *Whoopsee* . . .

It chose a clean path
through the middle of the train
shooting along as if
it had decided that instead
of being called a suitcase on wheels
it would call itself Thanatos.

The suitcase on wheels
(or Thanatos-on-wheels if you prefer)
full of exam papers hurtling
towards the end of the train.

It was as if my life-long myopia had lifted.
I could see everything with
such clarity, how beautiful it was to see!

How small that case
how redolent with sheen.

All that concentration. All that invigilation.

The end of the train opened
and the suitcase on wheels, *little Thanatos!*
dropped into the flames
as if it were a luminous detail
from that garden of earthly delights.

The University of Lanyard

Reasonable people are wearing lanyards. White collar ponies. *Clop! Clop*
How are you? I'm good. At what though? Actually, I'm rather good
at wearing a lanyard. I wear it on the way home, in the train. It's so,
well you know, corporate and lanyard-y. Don't you have one?
I did, I took it off and threw it away. Actually I popped it on
the neck of a goat. Or some long-haired prophet. Or maybe I stuck it up
the Dean's arse. Anyway I stack shelves now, or make lattes.
I have a tattoo on my inner thigh which says **A SEASON IN HELL**.
Even hell needs a lanyard. Hell is a lanyard. Love is a lanyard. God
is a lanyard. God is great. God is a neck-jiving, hip-swinging lanyard.

Exam Board

If I move my head I can feel the sun's warmth.

The External Examiner
hasn't finished speaking yet.

This Exam Board – November 25th
– 2015 – mid-afternoon – will end one day –

Praise be to God.

Even if the Chair
has conjured up the word Evangelise.

At the back of the room
a bowl of unripened fruit.

Help yourself Professor Finkelstein.
Help yourself Doctor Smallbone.

Neither does.

Farewell hard plum, ever uneaten.
Farewell hermetic, unyielding plum.

I want to say –

Today the flowers are blue
tomorrow there'll be kitchens of honey.

Hoy son flores azules . . .

I want to say –

To die, to sleep,
To sleep, perchance to dream; aye!

The External Examiner is becoming

the eternal examiner

Piss

You've written some poems
a play, a novel perhaps
and the thing you like about it
is the thing which wakes you
at three in the morning
with the fear that a sharp-toothed
animal is about to rip

out your heart. Weeks later
you're looking at the telephone
so carefully that it rings
and though you had hardly
imagined that it would happen
you had imagined it
and now it's happening.

A voice says, 'I'm handing you over
to Comrade Stalin.' You want to drop
the phone and run. Stalin says
Good morning comrade and you feel
a warm stream of piss down your leg.

Pull yourself together, you say to yourself
and then you make a noise which is supposed
to be a salutation. Stalin coughs.

When you open your mouth again
nothing comes out but a broken prayer:

Comrade Stalin,
I love you, you want to say,
because you are the poets' friend
who wrote poems in his youth,
excellent poems too, if I may say.

Then you weep.
You're weeping into the phone.
Comrade Stalin has called you
and you're weeping into the phone.

Revisionist, counter-revolutionary
enemy of the people weeping.

O God, let me weep in the right way.

Victor Hugo's Octopus

It wasn't friendly. Victor Hugo's octopus.
Circling the island like a spook.
It could speak French, a smattering of anglais.
It didn't have a hunch back, it didn't have a back.
It didn't give an SH one T about the subjunctive.
It said JE SUIS LE POULPE TERRIBLE DE VICTOR HUGO!

Its tentacles could surprise an early morning dog-walker.
Up they went over the cliff and the population
was reduced by one. This happened more and more.
Sheep and goats? Don't even mention them.
Dogs barked. Give them eight juicy bones said the magistrate
which was a lot. There was an argument at the Chief Pleas.
Perhaps the octopus required a sacrifice.
Perhaps we should give it that woman who runs the post office.
After all she's not that good at running the post office.
In actual fact I don't think we have a post office.

One evening an ex-cavalry man was taken off the cliff.
He shouted Death or Glory. Octopus crooned a chanson d'amour.
Sometimes the octopus slunk off to Herm
and just waited, a tactical retreat, almost Russian –
From Guernsey they sent a gunboat.
The octopus took it all the way down to the bottom of the sea.
Suck on that Palmerston.
Everyone edged a bit further to the centre

away from the coast, wild garlic proliferated.
The people of Little Sark created their own dialect.
The Seigneur started his memoir: *Please Don't Gulp My Blood.*

Shirley High Street

THE MUTANT MILE

I always thought the end of Shirley High Street
was the drop at the world's end. I know the maps
say differently but what are maps if not lies?
I tend to believe what I see with my eyes.
Shirley High Street is not without its horror –
I've seen Otto Dix weeping in Chicken City.
I've seen Otto Dix limping to the Chemist's.
He needed cod liver oil. He needed a bottle of *Cauchemar*.

If you walked to the end of the High Street you'd fall
off the world, that's what I thought, what's wrong with that?

It's a slow, exacting, Via Crucis.
A wailing wall, so many crazies in an urban wilderness.
Turkish barbers, Cash Converters, pawnbrokers.
Care in the community. Which means nothing.
I've seen a man with a bird cage on his head.
He had grown a beak. His eau de cologne
was Eau de Bird Shit, Eau de Mutant . . .
I've seen a gypsy leading a white mare.
It was the loveliest thing.
If you can travel to the heart of darkness
you can travel to the end of Shirley High Street.

I've seen Otto Dix harangued by a kebab.
I've seen Otto Dix wearing a gas mask.
For years I walked three quarters down, listened
to the ships' calls, listened to a wind

which wasn't a wind, a windless wind if you will.
It's not like Niagara Falls, no spray, nothing.
And then more nothing followed by nothing
followed by some Ravel, which is a boon.

Today I walked to the end of the road
and there was a shop selling parachutes.
I didn't buy one, I just carried on.
There was no drop. More of the same.
They just changed the name. Shirley High Street
became Coleridge Crescent. I wish there had been a drop.

I Know When To Stay In

Is that Mr Standard? the girl asks.
It's easier nowadays to say yes.
What sort of day are you having?
An average sort of day, I guess.
Oh that's nice, she says, I like average days.
Yes, I say, average is the new fantastico.
Average is the new Saturday night. Are you ready?
Mr. Standard! She laughs awkwardly.

I start quoting Davie Bowie
because he's quotable and because
he's dead. Davie Bowie is dead. Can that be true?
And who can bear to be forgotten? I say.
Mr Standard we won't forget you.
That's why we've rung you, we like ringing you.
Yes, I've noticed.

And then I say
Do you like pieces of machinery, mine shafts?
things like that? I've not given much thought
to mine shafts, I don't usually deal with them,
she says. Would you like to speak to my manager?
I don't want to speak to anybody.
Then I say, almost happy now,
I know when to go out, I know when to stay in,
get things done.

Mr Standard you're exactly
the kind of person we like, she says,
a throb in her voice. Thank you. And you know what?
What? she says. I feel tragic like I'm Marlon Brando.
Mr Standard, you really should speak to my manager,
his name's Keith. Scary monsters super Keith.
And then I say, my voice quite different now:
Oh my little China girl! Oh Mr. Standard! she replies.

Hey, you shouldn't mess me with me, I say,
I'll ruin everything you are. I'll give you television.
Television! Mr Standard, we're calling about
PPI – your Payment Protection Insurance.
Now listen here, I say, I stumble into town
like a sacred cow, visions of Swastikas in my head.

Dark Night of the Soul

Sometimes he goes away but then comes back.
Where have you been Henry?
Oh boy! he says, I had a dark night of the soul.

Henry doesn't do much, sometimes he practises
dance moves. Henry loves a good old fashioned waltz.
A spin me round the garden. Isn't life shiny? Isn't life short?

Sometimes he bobs along to the kitchen
and pecks on the glass door. May I come in?

Odd really, when you consider how many pheasants
end up in kitchens, including our kitchen,
roasted to perfection and let's open a bottle of wine.

You are the cream in my coffee, the salt in my stew.

When the door's open Henry walks in,
looks around, winkles his head, walks out.

Oof!

He's somewhat louche, a dandy
a French Symbolist perhaps, *oh là là*.

I make allowances.
Morning Henry. Fuck off, he says.

Sixty People with Flickering Lamps

Bury me at night
bury me in some English churchyard.

Let there be some crooning
Bessie Smith would do.

Let there be some Frederick Delius.

Let there be flasks of alcohol
let there be a clear-eyed manic bat,

and let there be a priest
hauled out of retirement.

Let there be something macaronic
a good old crack of the Teutonic.

Let there be Baron Osterhagen
with a gin and tonic.

Let there be a wooden cricket ball
let me swing low, sweet chariot.

From Warsaw to Krakow

I had forgotten the strange intimacy of European
travel, crammed into a compartment, my knees
touching the knees of the tall youth across the way
whose Slavic face I wanted to both slap and kiss,
his eyes as disturbing as the country I was travelling
through. When anyone returned from the lavatory
they carried their Weltschmerz with them. We opened
windows and the leaves came in and when the light
was fading bats too and Krakow only an hour away
with fields sloping and a trumpet and a blue house
and nothing mostly, miles of enervating nothingness,
which could, I guess, be the description of a life.

And the pigs? They'd fled to the capital
and camouflaged themselves between slices of bread.

The snug horror of the city and the countryside
full of lunatics and satanic mushrooms.

The train has changed its rhythm. I had been too shy
to read the poetry of Miłosz in front of my fellow travellers.
Seven pairs of eyes willing me to weep and shudder and throw
my head into my hands. The woman next to me lays down
her magazine – *More Stuff about Popes* – and reaches for a coat
which triggers off a strange dance as we pull down luggage
and dress and bump against each other for five or so
unchoreographed minutes, Silesian dumplings and religious
icons falling out of pockets. The Krakow train dance.

I haven't done it for years, the ecstasy!

Dross

I have some difficulty admitting this.
I'm not even sure how or why it happened
but it did, I'll have to come clean. Ah!
I watched *Valhalla Rising.*

Be kind –
I can't unwatch it now I've watched it.

Let me say how very late it was
and though I had no great desire to see it to the end
I had no great desire to go to bed.
In any case I wouldn't have slept
and would have had to lie there
in the dark listening to my heart
and switching on the light to read some Rimbaud.

Ah!

In case you haven't seen it
(this is my suggestion, keep it that way),
there's a lot of mud and heart surgery
without the slightest hint of anaesthetic
not even an axe to the head –
that comes later.

And it's the tenth century, talk about the sublime!
the weather is wretched most of the time

not a hint of summer till 1579.

You can be a Christian if you want –
(my god is better) or you can be a recalcitrant pagan:
My gods are many, I can eviscerate you.

There's a tree, a boring tree.

We could cut it down and make a fire
just to show we're post-Neanderthal then what?
Huddle round moon frog, no eye contact
and think to yourself, Holy shit, I'm still alive!
Small talk, unless you're an Abbot,
hasn't been invented.

Dialogue: actually there is some.
It's not exactly catchy
and the one-eyed Viking says absolutely nothing,
maybe he can't speak English
maybe the cat nabbed his tongue.

Viking tongue. Would you like some?

What do I know but I would say
all in all a low budget film:
bits of Scotland no one really likes
a river or two – mud,
things around people's necks,
a man with one eye
the Make Up Department going for it.

I'm not really into this stuff
but it was fairly obvious
you don't try and kill the one-eyed man,
don't even think about it,
especially when he's sleeping on a boat
which is supposed to be heading for the Holy Land
as if they'll just fetch up in Tel Aviv –
hey sunshine, oranges, what the hell are these?

It's like a bad horror film
when the young woman who's conveniently a virgin
says, I am just going to walk down that corridor
with a flickering candle even though
I have heard strange moaning sounds which
suggest that something horrible is going to happen to me
because I need to see the shutter is properly
fastened in the west wing, what with this wind.

Forget it, it's just a shutter,
go to your bedroom
and lock the door and if you need some distraction
read *Northanger Abbey*.
Then you're bound to nod off.

No, can't have the shutter banging
on a night like this.
I'll be alright, I have a candle.

Well, Fanny, don't say you haven't been warned –

silly bitch.

There, as we speak, werewolves, ogres, half-people
are walking across the heath because for reasons
known only to themselves they want to scoff some virgin
having first deflowered her unceremoniously.

Good luck, Fanny!

That flickering candle
and that clove of garlic down your pants
ain't going to help that much.

Good luck, Fanny!

You weren't very good at acting anyway.

Let's get back to *Valhalla Rising*.
I haven't mentioned it for a while.

There are some captured female slaves
all grouped together for a moment
and they're certainly not beauties
and they look bloody cold, why wouldn't they?

It's a film full of men –
standing there, fighting, looking, walking.
We've been in this bit of Scotland

for a while, let's go to another bit
even if it looks exactly the same:
we might see a sign, Jesus in a tree,
or someone's head on a long pole. Careful.

Men, men, men, without any structure to their lives:
just walking around looking bewildered or wise.

What do they do, all those men walking,
trekking off somewhere because someone
has pointed at a hill or a strange-looking bird
flying east? Look!

They can kill someone, that's allowed
especially in the tenth century,
actually any century will do.

Nork spills his seed in the wood.

Nork turns to Nanook
who's younger and has a pleasingly symmetrical face:

Bend over and show me your buttocks,
I know it's cold but it won't take long
and, you never know, you might like it.
I have a hunch (says Nork)
your buttocks are kinder than a tree.

When the one-eyed Viking is sleeping
on the boat, just sleeping it would seem,

and a soupy mist clings to the water
let's call it the whale road
the Christians think – We've got him,
let's slit his throat and pour his heathen blood
into the sea and Jesus will be happy and the mist
will lift and we'll reach Tel Aviv in an instant.

Who'll do it? I'll do it says this one.
No, I will, says another, getting up and unsheathing
his weapon. MISTAKE!

Even I know the one-eyed Viking isn't
really sleeping, he sees with his inner eye
and just as the man stoops the Viking has him.

There's a boy who looks on with awe.
The boy is safe because he's a boy
and he once gave the Viking something to eat.
The boy knows what the man is thinking.
He's an intelligent boy and no doubt will go far
not that you can go that far in the tenth century
although I suppose you could try Byzantium.

The one-eyed man fills the screen –
we are looking at his face
there is in fact nothing else to look at
not bad looking really
especially if you're into one-eyed men.
Oh sweet Viking!
There aren't any flies on him.

But, look again, there are! Some Viking flies!

What thou lovest well remains, / the rest is dross
What thou lov'st well shall not be reft from thee
What thou lov'st well is thy true heritage

I do in fact have the odd fly –
not sure why, even in winter
some fly flies in.

I don't mind really.

It's summer, the flies come in
doing nothing much.

You can't boss flies:
listen up, do as I tell you, wingèd thing.

It doesn't work that way.

I live on Shirley High Street.
It's terrible, the mutant mile.
Everyone limps, I limp too
to fit in, people limp on the mutant mile.

It's very late:

Valhalla Rising has been going on for hours.
This poem, too, is rather long.

The flies in my room are buzzing on the screen.
The flies are saluting the one-eyed Viking. Careful:
he might have you, snap, snap – nourishment.

I want to fly, should I take more Zoloft?
My cut-price airline.

There are flies on both sides of the screen!

There are Viking flies circling the one-eyed Viking
and there are flies at my end saluting their kinsfolk.

Humble Shirley flies, warrior Valhalla flies.

Everything has already happened.
Everything's been written.

Not this. Valhalla flies, the flies of Shirley.
A tryst of flies, the four horsemen, the four flies.
I think the world is about to end, oh please let it.

I would like to go to bed. Where's Nork?

Takeaway

I order an onion bhaji
and a chicken psychiatrist

and some bad music rice
and a rambutan tree.
and bung it on the Visa card.

Thank you Dr Standard.

When the food's delivered
I fish out the plastic bag

of chopped salad and lob it
elegantly into the bin.

The Glaswegian Book of Uncles

Al says, Do you want to listen to my
    uncle Bobby?
His iPhone has a crack along the glass.
I'm going to listen to a phone message.
Uncle Bobby is an ex-heroin addict
who got sent down for beating up
his girlfriend. Al was in the room,
Al was fourteen at the time; he called
the police. Uncle Bobby's forgotten
most things but he's not forgotten that.

I'm listening to uncle Bobby's
voice message, not much bonhomie.
He sounds like a bare knuckle fighter.
I expect he's good with his legs too.
What's the point of having legs
if you don't use them? – Go on Bobby
kick her, kick the dog, kick
your nephew, kick me if you like.

Actually, don't. I wish I hadn't said that.

I'm listening to uncle Bobby's voice message –
a message for his nephew Al.
I have never heard a message like that.
What if uncle Bobby knows I'm listening?

What if he stops and says –
Who's that fucking dobber listening in?
Glasgow to Southampton –

He could be here in a couple of hours.
Maybe uncle Bobby's packing his bag.
Hope the sniffer dogs sniff him out.

There are more than sixty million people in the UK.
Hope I don't have to meet uncle Bobby.

(Al's granddad thought it a kind of miracle
when Al went to college, a degree in social work.

It's not as if the family didn't need a social worker,
what with Al's brother being in prison and Al

spending years in care, not to mention uncle Bobby
and the other stuff and now Al was becoming
a social worker . . .)

Al says, When I was in care
I would pray to God to make my arse nicer.

– it was a plate of bones!

I imagine he gets loads
of requests like that, I say.

Al is staring at his phone.

Anyway, I continue, it seems
as if he intervened on your behalf.

Thanks, Al says, I appreciate that.

He's texting uncle Bobby.
Stay in fucking Glasgow he writes.

Go back to prison ya cunt.

Billings to Minneapolis

And she used to write poetry, oddball stuff, it didn't rhyme
or anything and it certainly didn't make much sense and
they gave her electro-shock therapy and she went crazy,
maybe she was already crazy, she just went crazier,
I guess, and even lovelier.

It brought the freckles out, the crazed girl with freckles.
Have you had electric shock therapy? No, I say –
not yet. My advice, says Frank, is not to have it. It didn't do
Haley any good and, as far as I know, she never wrote
another word just a blank page for ever,
a blank page for the whole of life, Frank says. I used
to watch her sometimes, she'd pick up this pen of hers
and write on that page, as if she owned it – that was

before they plugged her in – she was good, I mean good with
words, they just came out like she had a secret supply
that no one else could get to. And she made weird noises
when we were making out, really weird. I guess it comes
with the territory, Frank says. The weird noises, you mean?

He nods. Do you make weird noises? he asks. I do sometimes.
That's OK, he says, I'm fairly broad-minded when it comes to it.
The stewardess comes with pretzels, cookies and wet towels.
High in the American sky, in a place that's nowhere.
I kind of like it: my private pretzel paradise.

You know, said Frank, I can ride bulls from one end of
America to the other but I couldn't do fuck all with a blank
page. To be honest, it'd scare the shit out of me. If I were in

a Kansas Motel alone with some smart arse blank page I might
even go and shoot somebody. Well, I say hesitantly, looking at
the battered cowboy, the blank page can be troublesome but
I don't think you can compare it with a buck off.

He puts up a hand. Listen, did you tell me your name? I think
you did but I've forgotten it – anyway I've broken every damn
bone in my body and I know you're suffering,
you've broken those bones that no one else can see. Come on
man, admit it, it's in your face, it's in your dumb questions.
And you know what, I respect you for that –

we're both broken, broken differently, I guess, broken
in different ways, broken men on a plane that's being flown by
a broken Vietnam vet who reads Walt Whitman in a log cabin
full of peacock shit in the middle of some gloomy transcendental
forest. Thank you I say, eating another pretzel (they're so good!)
And then we look out of the window, that's what it's for,
it's mostly cloud, and more cloud.

Between Opalescence and Obsession

is a word I swore I'd never use
neither in a poem nor for that matter
in any other kind of document.
And now I've broken my word – I'm sorry.
Hope the sky won't drip with blood.

Consider, for example, the much maligned,
unfairly as it turns out, Emperor Obsidian
who was cruelly savaged by a pack of dogs.
Not to mention the embattled years of that
little known Secretary of State, Jack Obsidian.

And – be careful now! – the illegitimate son
of Queen Victoria – the Marquis D' Obsidian –
who threw himself into steam trains and then

moved out to Missoula. And that recently
published memoir by what's his name –
that world famous palaeontologist?
A real page turner: *My Life of Hope with Obsidian.*
And let's not forget those foot-stamping years:
Count Beauchamp and his Obsidian Blues.

Yes, I'm stirred with a strange enthusiasm.
Let me introduce you to my first born:
I've called him Obsidian the Terrible,
the first of many I'm almost certain – Rejoice!

Turkey Blues

There were nice admin ladies in the Liberal Arts Building.
They wanted to know if I'd seen the campus turkeys.
Do they sing to you in the morning? Awake Visiting Professor!
There's no need for an alarm clock when you have
a phalanx of swaggering turkeys fornicating on the college lawns.
Time to wash and dress – high fives for getting dressed – and
time for an American breakfast: a plate of waffles? scrambled
eggs? and coffee which doesn't taste like coffee yet so much of it.
Then walk in a professorial manner to the tower
which is like a beige smack across the face. It's almost bracing.

I had noticed there were no windows on the turkey side
but had imagined, if I'd imagined anything, that the light
of Montana would push through elsewhere like a victory
snatched out of the jaws of defeat, like the cavalry turning up
to rescue Custer at the battle of Little Big Horn.

The last idiosyncratic throes of modernism. Le Corbusier on a
bad day and Monsieur Le Corbusier had, I believe, several bad days.
Or maybe the workers forgot to put the windows in.
They were distracted, they were in love, or they just weren't
very good at doing their job.

In any case they had crossed into North Dakota before anyone had
taken stock. Gentlemen, there's a great deal of brick, six floors of it,
but no windows. Zany, cool even, and so liberal –
a Liberal Arts Building without the dictatorship of light!
I'm going to freak out and write a paper on Paul de Man.

Boom Boom Boom Boom I'm gonna shoot you right down,
  right off your feet . . .

I feel like Louis Theroux. He's talking to a serial murderer in a prison
cage who's shaved and full of tattoos. He has strangled several women
with astonishing brutality but has recently found God even if God
wasn't doing much to be found. How many more years have you got?
I reckon I've got about 300 years. Gosh, that's quite a lot, says Louis
and in the silence that follows you wonder whether the born again
serial murderer might put his arm through the bars and grab the
Englishman by the throat if only to knock the blankness off his face.

I'm talking to Professor Schnabel who has spent thirty years teaching
Romantic Literature. What's it like, I ask, teaching Keats in a building
without light? It's a figure of speech says the professor
and life would be intolerable without figures of speech.

Free range Tom Turkeys and their sassy paramours wobble around
the campus drunk on light and happy with the knowledge
they will never have to write an essay on *The Great Gatsby*
or *The Infernal Desire Machines of Dr Hoffman*.
And they don't give a coyote for the Futurist Manifesto – our speed,
they say, is perfect as they bustle towards the statue of Crazy Horse.
Sometimes they wonder what happens in the building without light
  and shudder.

One of the turkeys has a guitar, the others gather round,
he's singing the Turkey Blues.
Up in the mountains there are bears and elk and moose and wolves
and trees dripping with snow.

Boom Boom Boom Boom I'm gonna to shoot you right down, right
off your feet, take you home with me and put you in my house –
And in my house, sings some teenage joker, *there are windows*
    throughout!

And they keel over with laughter, some of them are actually weeping.

I'm talking to the sisters – identical twins – professors of linguistics
and they're all ginsenged up. Who needs light when you're blessed
with the inner light? I'm Miss Mood, says the one with dark framed
spectacles and I'm Miss Lexicon says the other
whose spectacles are as dark framed as her sister's – perfectly
interchangeable I guess.

Have you seen the turkeys? Yes. Have you, by chance, noticed
the window situation? Yes. They nudge each other. He's one smart cookie,
and then they laugh. We all laugh. When there was a quake in Oklahoma,
they tell me, the building without windows moved.

I reckon, Miss Lexicon says, the guy who designed the building also
designed Correctional Facilities and the Dean that year was having
some kind of spiritual crisis – and it was cheaper without windows
in any case, and no sign the war in Vietnam was finishing any time soon.

Maybe it had something to do with redemption.
It's not a metaphor, it's a pedagogical nightmare and we've been given
life sentences. It's like *Bleak House* but much longer and much bleaker,
no canaries released from any cages.

Oh hell, I say.

[37]

Miss Mood says that might be true but she has another theory,
however she's got a class so will have to tell me later.
See you later alligator. In a while crocodile.

When I'm alone in the Alumni House lying on a bed that could sleep
half the football team watching *Buck Off Special* at the Billings Bull Ri
    Spring Testicle Buck Off Festival
I hear a voice in my head which insists on being listened to.

And one day
        Boom Boom Boom Boom
                I'm going to write it all down.

The Crucible

I dream of being that snooker player whose opponent
is so masterful there's nothing doing but to sit alone
in one's sartorial splendour occasionally sipping a glass of water
knowing that the camera is zooming in to investigate
your existential gloom, listening to the click of ball on ball
and the ripple of applause which accompanies your opponent's
unassailable lead. One needs to look the part, in defeat
as well as victory, certain that the pundits are making sly remarks
or even revealing a sudden sympathy for your spluttering career,
one of the best dressed players on the circuit, they're thinking,
yet one of the least successful.

You realise that you're actually fond of the sitting position,
a ring side view is not without advantages:
you find yourself remembering a wind in the trees and somewhere
there's a beach and the black sliding into its pocket is perfection,
even a kind of death. You're unexpectedly happy and you want
to hug your opponent, not just shake his hand; you want to hug him
like a brother, like a friend, like a lover, and the coloured balls
remind you of a Mexican Fiesta even though they've long slunk off
into the undergrowth. You feel like Siegfried or a workman
who's finished his shift at last – the sitting shift – who can now
lie down and relax and drink something stronger than water.

In fact you can't wait to kick off your shoes and the table is like
a manicured lawn – Please Keep Off – but now that you've lost
so stylishly, so effortlessly, you're going to lie down
on the grass, certain they will forgive you this indulgence,
given that you've spent so much time banished from the garden.
You can hang yourself with a tie but a bow-tie is like a fig leaf

which covers up your shame and because you've suffered such
a staggering defeat you're going to take it off and that's just the start.
You remember the wind and the beach and you're running free,
a trail of clothes behind you – naked, blissful, snookered.

I Can Feel You

Call the mole-catcher. He's dead.
Oh good. I mean good for the moles.
The whole of this side of England
is trembling. Veronica has a theory:
They're Dutch moles, they're good
at digging, the last time they came
was 1688, the Glorious Revolution
of the Moles. Do you remember?
There'll be windmills everywhere
and we'll have to eat that awful cheese
and clean the road outside our house.
And, says Cherry, speak a language
which absolutely nobody can understand.
We'll get used to it, says Veronica
and I do like an open sandwich.
And the Dutch are very tall. She's looking up.

She ought to be looking down:
mole hills, moles, unending voluptuousness.
Not a mole-catcher in the whole of
East Anglia. Either they've gone mad
or been carted off to Bletchley Park.

You thought the war was over –
that's what they call trick photography.
The war's still on! Round up the mole-catchers
and let moles have a prolonged period of ecstasy.

I'm lying on my mother's lawn
which has been hijacked by mole heaps.
Oh moles I can hear you
under the ground, reading extracts
from *The Monk* by Matthew Lewis
and doing a little free-style rap.

I can feel you, I can feel you.
I'm lying still looking at the sky.
Is that a Spitfire or an oyster-catcher?
Is it neither one nor the other?
Oh moles, I can feel you.

I can feel you.

Pigs in Suffolk

Unlikely Troubadours,
knights without armour,
the Arthurian legends
which Mallory forgot –
sizzling comets
falling from the sky!

I like the way they hang out
in pig camps, wide-open fields
with bungalows.

They all seem to bump
along together, taking their
mud baths, cheering at
the orchestra. Oh ring it out,
the perfect pork note!

And playing chess.
Did you know a Suffolk sow
gave Bobby Fischer
a run for his money?

Oh, you speak so highly
of them it makes me think
you'd like to come back

as a pig!

Maybe, if only for a day.

I'd like to arrange
my magisterial flanks
under the sky.

I'd like to jab
my snout
almost anywhere.

Toby's Singing

What a glorious feelin'
I'm happy again –
I'm laughing at clouds,
and I'm ready for love.

It is raining.
This is June 2016 and this is England.
We have voted to leave Europe.
Goodbye sweet continent
of happy food and happy sunshine
and finely-balanced subjunctive clauses.

I'm ready for love, sings Toby,
I'm singing in the rain.
We're all singing in the rain
or rather we're not singing
in the rain, we're just standing
in the rain listening to Toby.

Seagulls clatter, swoop, hover,
or stand on the gazebo and they too
are singing – We're ready for love
and blah de blah de blah in the rain
'cos we're English seagulls
and we love the bleeding rain.

In Aldeburgh the tea rooms are full
of people eating scones
and being nostalgic about the Blitz.
Wasn't it marvellous, they say
the way we sang and carried on?

We pulled ourselves up by the bootstraps
and shoved an inordinate amount
of pork pie and skate wing down our throats.

Monica says, vis-à-vis the seagulls,
(Monica's writing a YA novel and comes
from Melbourne) They're drones!
I know you'll find that's a bugger to believe
but I've done my research, tedious
amounts of it, and those sea gulls swooping
and swaying and going backwards and
shitting in the wind are bloody drones.

Heat Wave

My body is a text, I like to illustrate.
I thought your body was a body.
I can give you paper if you like.
My body is a manuscript of medieval vellum.
I am a walking palimpsest, a hermeneutic
cabaret. I'm available for close readings.
How closely would you like to be read?
If I revealed all you might have an epiphany.
Oh one of those, I said, they seem to be
occurring all over London.
No one loves a thin Falstaff, he said.

And football isn't coming home, Football said.

Charles Boyle Baudelaire is throwing a party
in Shepherd's Bush and I'm talking to a taxi driver
from the Horn of Africa.
(I rather like saying the Horn of Africa.)
The driver who is Somalian is complaining
about the heat.
In Mogadishu we have exquisite breezes.
I doubt we'll have many in Shepherd's Bush.

Christopher is lying on a sofa
in the cool of the house.
I was about to faint, he says –
we're all about to faint, I say, there, look, we've fainted!
Water, water, a glass of cordial perhaps?

A lady in white holds an oriental parasol
in the garden and leans forward
to wipe the face of Henry James Horovitz.

I'm talking to a Spanish poet who can't hear.
We get two beer cans and a piece of string
and she stands on one side of the garden
and I stand on the other.

Can you hear me now? I ask.
Nada, she says, absolutely fucking nada.

Kim

Just one of those things –
the pundits sighing and spluttering
getting the right angle on the blue.

I've not seen anything like it. Don't put the kettle on.
How to Make your Home Perfect (imagine that?)
has been re-scheduled. Whoever takes this frame
is in the final. There's a lot of money riding on this.

A puff of the cheeks. A shake of the head,
the tongue venturing out to caress the lips.
Steve Turnover. He's taking it on! What a shot!
You'd never imagine this was the deciding frame.
You can't keep an old dog muzzled.
Is he hampered? Is he waiting the postman's knock?
Will he promote the pink? It's hit and hope. It's shit or bust.

The camera pans to the seated Kim.
He's like a loaf of bread. Has he played his last shot?
You've got to give it to him. Ten years ago he was heading up
a failed dictatorship, his fingers on the nuclear button.

Now he's reached the world snooker semi-finals at the Crucible.
He's an inspiration, his safety play has come on
leaps and bounds. And all those years in northern towns
as an amateur, dodging hitmen from the DPR.

Steve Turnover, all said and done, has yet to cross the line.
Puff of the cheeks. A little shake of the head.
He will be feeling it – make no mistake.

HE'S MISSED IT COMPLETELY!
Kim might well have a sniff of something now.

SETTLE DOWN PLEASE.

He's a popular player on the circuit
with his trademark haircut and Pyongyang suits
(his arms not long enough to reach the far off ball,
his legs too short to wrestle with the Spider.)

And you couldnae make up the story of his defection . . .

He took the Great Leader's train to Vladivostok,
an international meet with Putin, got back on the train
and directed it through Siberia to Moscow.
He travelled under cover of darkness, undetected mostly.
The Americans got a tip off.

It turned out the green train had a snooker table
as well as a carriage full of lobster and dancing girls
and Kim Jung-un had many hours of practice.
A boyhood dream, he never really enjoyed being a dictator.

This frame's still hanging in the balance.
*You knew when Kim came back to the table
he wasn't going to say nowt to bloody owt.*

This is a massive shot – yellow, pink, not much available.
Kim Dug-in Kim Jung-un the former dictator
with a chance of making it to the finals of the World Championship.

SETTLE DOWN PLEASE!

From Moscow the green train slid into Vienna.
Kim wanted to see some Klimt, Egon Schiele.
He played chess in Budapest and then Berlin for a cabaret.
He wanted to let his hair down, not that he had much.

Paris in the spring, Kim visited Les Invalides
and the Boat Train to Dover. Asylum, debriefings,
phone calls from the White House.

Apart from his batman – Dong-woo, a snooker player no less –
Kim struck out alone, leaving his entire entourage in Margate
including a Field Marshal.
Snooker table after snooker table, small hotels, Blackpool –
ineffectual disguises, a smattering of English
      with a strange northern accent.

Can he avoid the double kiss? Can he avoid the postman's
knock? Can he avoid the double agent? What more has he got
in his locker? There's a gap. *There's always a gap.*
Kim needs to get lucky – he's desperate for a piece of luck.
If Kim pots this he's in the final.

SETTLE DOWN PLEASE! It's hit and hope, *it's shit or bust . . .*

An Itch in the City

A purple slipper in the street

An itch in the city

A bishop in flight –

Bushel

Whosoever invented the chair, God bless him.
And the floor, what would we do without the floor?
And the man who invented the door, I salute you.
I guess it was a man, busy and bearded
and his saying to no one in particular, The hinge!
And the wife saying, What on earth is that?
It's a door, I have invented one. Now what?
You may slam it if you like. The man goes through
the door and walks into a wood. Well done that inventor
of woods! It was Dante I think, what a breakthrough
that was. And the corridor. Too little has been said
about the inventor of corridors. Stop hiding
your light under a bushel. A bushel?
I know who invented the bushel, hah!
And the handkerchief! Imagine a life without
handkerchiefs! And windows are cool,
all those people, moving around. Madame Omelette,
wherever you are, you should pat yourself
on the back too. We stand in awe, come now,
a game of Six-Egg-Snooker then at last
the weight taken off those feet. You may sit down.
In fact, we can all sit down. It's beautiful.

Boxing Day

The dogs are going crazy.
I think mother slipped them
some amphetamines.

A truly enormous ham
is being cooked

and the dogs are becoming idiotic and psychotic.

My ex-wife is late which is good
and not so good. Mother pulsates.

Welcome ex-wife, have some ham.
I watch Mother slicing slicing slicing.
Two pieces of ham for ex-wife,
and three pieces of ham for me.

O Bethlehem!

O Bethlehem!

In England we eat boiled ham, Mother says.
Do you like boiled ham? Mother asks ex-wife.
Ex-wife says, I have been to West Ham,
I may have taken the wrong line.

After the enormous ham
Mother shouts, Pudding!
and off she walks to the special shed.

I am left with ex-wife.
Shall we dance? No.

Water has flowed under the bridge,
says ex-wife. Not enough I'm thinking.

Flee whilst you can, ex-wife! Flee!

Mother's walking back to the house,
the dogs have conked out
in some post-amphetamine afternoon lock-down.

Mother appears with a trifle.
An enormous trifle.
In England, Mother says, we eat trifle.

Berrylands

Where John Ashbery
never got round

to visiting the fruit trees
which don't exist –

where Trotsky never created
a revolutionary cell

where the trains slap by
to Clapham Junction

where the trains slap by
to Clapham Junction

where Oscar stood
in penitentiary clothes

and the crowd enjoyed
his humiliation.

There's a beautician in Berrylands
called Chantelle

she's good at fornication –

There a café in Berrylands
called The Weltschermz

which specialises
in not being open.

A pit bull terrier
makes love to my ear –

her salacious tongue.

My sleep patterns
are all shot through.

If I dream at all
I dream of somewhere far-flung.

I dream of Mogadishu.

Any Tickets Please?

How good to have a ticket
and then be asked to show one!

The man's hirsute arm leans across me
and then he doodles on the ticket.
The Kurt Schwitters of South West Rail.

Calvin Harris says:
These are the good times of your life.

Trolley Man

When someone asks, Could I have
a sandwich with some cheese in it?
I will say No sandwiches today!

And if anyone should ask for coffee
I will say, Hot water not working.
Shocking, isn't it?

I will wheel my trolley from one end
of the train to the other, smiling
magnificently at everyone.

And when a lady asks,
I don't suppose you've got
a piece of shortbread
some lovely, lovely shortbread?

I will say, No my dear
all the lovely shortbread has gone.

Glasgow/ Six of One

I'm at Buchanan Street,
I need to get to Ibrox.
I could take the Inner Circle
or I could take the Outer.
It's six of one, it's half a dozen of the other.

It's six of one,

               half a dozen of the other.

I'm at St Enoch
I need to get to Partick.
I could take the inner circle, or I could take the outer.

It's six of one, half a dozen of the other.

I'm skint. I need to borrow money.
I could ask JP, or I could ask Jon.

It's half a dozen of the other, it's six of one.

My heart is dry, as dry as wood.

There are things I shouldn't do.
There are things I should.

(I really ought to phone my mother . . .)

I could turn to Jesus
or I could turn to Allah.

It's six of one, it's half a dozen of the other.

Seven Sisters

They were good Catholics, distantly related, it was said, to
the Duke of Norfolk. And they had six girls. Who were inseparable.
The six sisters, a talking-point, a trove. Only sister number three,
the most modest, married. Her husband was a general
who smelt of talcum powder. In the confines of their
Wiltshire home he had an unhealthy interest, complained Dorothy
in one of her letters, in the Turkish penchant for sodomy
and sherbet. In fact, she wrote to her sisters asking them
whether a wife needed to satisfy such Byronic appetites.
The sisters, virginal of course, considered the situation and
suggested that if married life were such an ordeal she should return
to the fold and leave the general to his sherbet. Dorothy packed
her bags and left whilst her husband was drinking at his club.

                                                    As for the rest
it would take a novel, not exactly a page turner, to chart the moves
and desires of these catholic women, all educated, with commendable
occupations and eager to give to the world, a world which had always
regarded them with affection. Suffice to say, and one notes a pleasing
strangeness here, that in the middle part of their lives the six sisters
bought a spacious property in Seven Sisters, in the north of London.

It was about that time, only partly cognisant of the matter
(my mother had begun the story on several occasions . . .), I booked
an Uber taxi for Seven Sisters. I needed to go to the station.
It was, in theory, a ten minute journey from Warwick Grove.
The driver was a woman whose English wasn't good and
she seemed confused even angry, asking me to confirm my
destination and I pointed out (again) I wanted Seven Sisters Station.
She was looking at her Uber map and pointed to what appeared to be

the Seven Sisters district of Hong Kong. Gosh, I said,
how much would that cost? Haringey to Honk Kong! Book
another taxi, she said and she went – shouting something derogatory
in Spanish. Seven sisters, Hong Kong, I was suddenly overtaken
by a peculiar feeling and decided to google it. Tsat Tsz Mui Road,
Seven Sisters Road, was named in memory of the sisters'
collective leap into the South China Sea. Committed to chastity
they carried out this group suicide in protest against the
enforced marriage of sister number three. Next day, the story has it,
seven boulders, each shaped like a woman, were washed up against
the shore. I ought to add, as if perhaps I'd forgotten, that as a
boy I had lived in Hong Kong. My father was a colonel who smelt
of Old Spice and Tiger Balm. And one Christmas

my sister came out from London bringing her betrothed.
Sundays we walked down to the sea past the Repulse Bay Hotel,
and the courting couple wandered away among the rocks. I had,
by now, booked another taxi but not before my google
searches had thrown up an ancient lithograph called Bugan Cifu –
Not Willing To Bend Over As A Female – which shows
a courtesan dressed in male clothing . . . What an interesting
morning I was having! Yasin arrives
in a Toyota Prius and we start chatting. He's from Ethiopia
and we get onto Haile Selassie and Rastafarianism. Yasin says
he doesn't think he was God's prophet, just
a man of blood and bones, but anyway there's a place in
Ethiopia where the Rastas live. Now we are passing through
Stamford Hill and the streets are full of Hasidic Jews.
Yasin – a Muslim – says he likes Jews – they don't drink,
they don't vomit in his taxi, they work hard and the women are

respectable. He points to a woman pushing a pram:
she's beautiful, he says, she's on benefits. He seems to know
everyone in Stamford Hill but isn't sure where the station is.
Excuse me he says, winding down his window –
he's talking to a black woman in a black dress –
where's the station sister? And I'm thinking of Pirandello's
other play – *Seven Sisters in Search of a Station* –
but it's only a passing thought because there it is, and I'm pulling
out my case and Yasin's laughing and putting his thumbs up.

It's a nice bright October day and there's a white sheet on my
sister's washing line. It's enormous and it seems to block the house
and create a curtain at what might be some strange theatre –
or a sailing ship in repose, the sail now limp before a wind
that's kicking up over the horizon. I am full of peace.

Bus Replacement 2

It's almost two in the morning
and you find yourself at Eastleigh.
There are three buses and scores
of miserable people, many with suitcases.
The drivers in a circle, smoking.

Is this one going to Bournemouth? I ask.
It might be mate, I'm just the driver, how should I know?

Another man leans across, You could take
the white bus, that's my one, but I wouldn't advise it.
I don't like driving in the dark because
I'm blind in one eye and fuzzy in the other.

In any case the buses aren't going anywhere yet
because another round of cigarettes is required
and the drivers are tired and they're not real drivers
anyway, just somebody's uncles standing in –
smoking cheap fags and telling bad jokes.

A young man carrying a rucksack shouts
I have a gun and I'm going to shoot myself!
and we turn on him like an angry mob.
You're so selfish! Why not shoot us first,
one by one, and then rock off to Valhalla, *Valhalla*?
I don't have enough bullets, he says.

Don't worry about that says the one-eyed driver,
I've got a stash of them at the back.
Great we say, that's sorted then, and the drivers

are pleased too because they won't have to go anywhere. No point going to Bournemouth with a cockeyed bullet in your head.

Snazzy

Cherry's left a snazzy hoover under the stairs,
Mother says. Could you take it out for a spin?
I have a good look at it. It looks like a Dalek.
It might have been 'snazzy' in 1995.
I manage to turn it on. The room says Oh really?
Mother's in the kitchen doing something
with the Christmas Ham. Oh Bethlehem! Oh Bethlehem!
Hoover must have been bored under the stairs.
Now it's going for it:
bits of snazzy Dalek are shooting all over the place:
tubes, small brushes, unexpected ejaculations.

How's it going? Mother shouts. Great, I say
as Dalek mashes up the Bokhara rug
and the dogs bolt up the stairs.
Too late to stop now.
In any case the off switch doesn't seem to work.
My ex-wife's coming round for Boxing Day Ham
and mortification.
Don't want the place to look like a tip.

Hoover drags me into the kitchen
where Mother, Ham, and ex-wife (surprisingly early,
she must have come round the back . . .)
appear like a triptych.
Dalek makes a terrifying sucking noise
and I watch Mother, Ham and ex-wife
disappear into the capacious bowels
of Cherry's snazzy hoover. I am a middle-aged man:
I am afraid of nothing.

Eau Sauvage

for Charles

Richard John Bingham, 7th Earl of Lucan (born 18 December 1934; presumed dead), commonly known as Lord Lucan, was a British peer suspected of murder who disappeared in 1974.

I get an unexpected
text from Lord Lucan:

Will you read my poems?
Yes, Lord Lucan, I will.

Tomorrow, when I look
for the message it isn't

there – I mean his part
of the message isn't there.

Just, Yes Lord Lucan I will.
It sounds like a song.

Yes, Lord Lucan, I will.
Yes, Lord Lucan, I will.

A week later a package
drops through the letter box –

22 Landguard Road
into a communal hallway,

full of envelopes
addressed to neighbours

who've long since disappeared:
Miss Moon, Miss Pinkerton

Miss Reckless, Miss Raven

and the loveliest of all
Miss Craven.

I read the poems
with trembling lips.

I read the poems
with trembling thighs.

I read the poems
with widening eyes

and then ring Charles Boyle
ex-poet of Shepherd's Bush.

Is that Charles Boyle
ex-poet of Shepherd's Bush?

Yes, says Charles
as – indeed – you well know.

I want to find the right *ton*

I want to suggest
that in a previous life

I rubbed shoulders
with interesting people.

A little hushed, throaty, I say,
The poems of Lucan have landed.

What are you talking about?
says Charles, are you demented?

I think you should take a look.
I think you should publish the book.

Actually, I rather enjoy thinking
of Charles Boyle in Shepherd's Bush.

Charles says, Read me a couple,
read me a poem by Lucky Lord Lookey.

Read me, read me. Alright, alright.
I'm sifting through the poems

and the room is zinging with
the aroma of Eau Sauvage

Read me a couple, read me a couple.

I'm reading them to myself.
I'm not reading them to Charles.

I'm reading them to myself.
They're so louche and so elegant

so decadent and so intelligent.
In fact they're not poems at all.

They're too good to be poems.
It's like putting one's hand in a glove.

It's like smoking a little Tina
Bonjour little Tina. Bonjour.

They're not poems at all.

Poems which are better than poems
ought to be called something other

than poems. Read me a couple
says Charles, read me a couple of poems

that are better than poems.

Charles is making a strange noise
at the end of the phone.

I have the most extraordinary
non-poems in the world

and Charles is making a noise
at the end of the phone.

The ex-poet of Shepherd's Bush
the most insouciant publisher

in the city of London
the most audacious publisher

in the city of London
the most charming publisher

in the city of London
is making a strange noise

at the end of the phone.

Oh read me a couple.
Oh read me a couple.

No! No! No!
And then I pretend
someone's knocking

at the door.

In fact I go to the door
and start knocking on it

knock, knock, knock:
Charles, I say, someone's knocking

at the door – You'd better
answer it, he says.

I think he might be thinking
it's Lovely Lord Lucky.

Knock, knock, knocking
at the door.

Who's knock knock
knocking at the door?

Virginia Woolf

Miss Photo-Synthesis

Frederick Seidel

Charles Manson

Charles Boyle

Not even Charles
can be in two places
at the same time –

Professor Kiss

Miss Reckless

Arthur Rimbaud
with only one leg

Salvador Dalí

Lord Lucan

alleged killer of Nannies,

holding some
lead pipe and

a mediocre bottle
of vodka.

Oh Lord Lucan

is knocking at the door!
(Obviously he isn't,

I'm putting on a
show for Charles!)

Hang on a moment, I say
walking round the room

in a euphoric circle.
Hang on a moment, I say

walking round the room
in a euphoric circle.

Sweet Lord – sweet Lord
someone *is* knocking

at the door!

I mean someone
who is not me –

someone who is not me!

The jazz police are leaning
on my shoulders.

The Poetry Foundation
is going through my folders.

Blah, blah de blah

blah

Charles is making a strange noise
and someone's knocking at the door.

And I have seen enough
black and white films

to know that the person
in the shit – which happens to be me

(how did that happen?)

needs to be fleet of foot
and I would be happy

to flush the poems – I haven't
yet thought of another name –

for the poems other than *poems* –
down the lavatory:

the flusher is a spitter
rather than a flusher

the flusher is a spitter
rather than a

I called the plumber
a hundred times.

His name is Trevor.
Oh, he's subtle.

I called the plumber
a hundred times.

I know he's there

at the end of the phone
feigning a psychotic attack

in the back of his van.

You can stick your little pins
in that voodoo doll.

I cannot flush
the Lucan poems.

I cannot burn the Lucan poems
not a log in sight.

OPEN UP! OPEN UP!

Lord Lucky has written
his poems on exquisite

parchment and I realise now
I will have to eat them.

That's what they do in France
when the Gestapo comes

knocking on the

        door.

The young woman who
everybody loves drinks

a glass of Beaujolais

and swallows the name
of the agent which slips down

her throat

and lies in the pit of her stomach.
We know the Gestapo

will not break her –
they will torture her

and they will kill her.
She will die, having

swallowed the name

of a very important agent.
She will save France.

They will not break her.
There will be a statue of her

in Rue Julien-Lacroix
Je ne regrette rien/ everything.

I am now eating the poems
of Lord Lucan

what a pity he wrote so many!

The Gestapo are knocking
at the door

and I am eating the poems
of Lord Lucan.

Eat eat eat.

Eat eat eat.

And I say – in a muffled voice
I'm coming! I'm coming!

Give me some extra moments
Meine Herren

I'm just getting out of the shower!
As if.

I called the plumber
a hundred times.

Maybe I should pretend
I am merely a piece of paper

and rustle, rustle
or maybe I should just lie doggo

        for a while –

I'M COMING! I'M COMING!

I don't want the Gestapo
to think I'm some

dirty, unwashed poet
floating on the Oh là là

of drug-fuelled auto-erotica

so I'm dabbing
my neck with Eau Sauvage

and slipping on
the silkiest of dressing gowns

as if I'd just been putting
the final touches to

Blithe Spirit

Dabbing on a little Eau Sauvage.

Eat eat eat.

Eat eat eat.

I'm coming! I'm coming!

Z took Lucy the Dog to Work

and I stayed at home
and became the dog.

I can scamper along the terrace
as much as I like
but I can't open the fridge with my nose.
Z turned the fan off (why?)
It's very hot
and the floor has become folded
into the reality of my unwished-for transformation.

Do dogs care about ceilings much?

I think Z is trying something out
which is why she got some biological yoghurt
and said Have a Nice Day in the way she said it.

Have a Nice Day! (soon to be a dog, hahaha,
a Lucy dog, a Chinese Crested Variety,
a deluxe doppelgänger thingamajig,
even perhaps, we will judge later, a dog-poet.)

I don't know where to pee.
I was reading *The Strange Death of Europe*
and being a dog it's hard to read now
and I'm finding it quite hard to write this.
A bit dashed off, I feel, with a slightly unpleasant smell.

Lucy is a bitch – a Chinese Crested Variety –
and that's what I've become.
Cocking my leg was the wrong manoeuvre.

If there were a good sized handbag around
I could jump into it and that would be that.

At this moment the other Lucy,
deluxe doppelgänger thingamajig human variety,
is walking on two feet
and buying bream in the fish market.
She likes shopping (the bitch!)

I tried to bark and something came out
which sounded like Iggy Pop.
We'll ride through the city tonight –
(oh yes!), see the city's ripped backsides.

Bollocks and Teeth

Elmo jumped out of the car,
all bollocks and teeth.
Concetta scrambled onto the roof.

Luigi keeps tortoises.
He has about ten
including a Sardinian one
called Fish Sandwich.

The males are highly sexed.
They queue up behind the female,
a tortoise gang-bang.

The Sardinian is female
but they don't seem to like her.
Hers, therefore, is a life of chastity.
An anchorite in a shell.

All shall be well,
and all manner of thing shall be well.

If only.

Elmo is drooling and snarling.
He wants tortoise.

We tell Daria to put him
back in the car and Daria says
he wouldn't hurt a fly
which is a blatant untruth.

Elmo is at his happiest
when he has something in his mouth:
an arm, a leg, a chair, a tortoise,
even – why not? – an anchorite.

The Road to Bastardo

You can eat from any tree
but not the one which yields
the figs. We ate plentifully,
the juice running down our chins.
A car pulled up. *Questa la strada
per Bastardo?* Yes, yes, we said
and wandered back to Daria's car –

sweet now with figs
and she drove fast across Umbria –
I haven't killed anyone yet
and would like to keep it that way.

Vineyards. Olives. Dust.

Monte Fucking Falco she cries out.
Then adds, I want to make a risotto
and have a line of Carrara White
if there were such a thing
or Umbrian Crystal or Spoleto Blue.
How would you get that up your nose?

Elmo the dog is eating a chair: yum-yum

and the stars are out and someone's
on the tower, the Duke of what's his name,
the Duke of weird shit is dancing
the Thirteenth Century Templar Blues
with a goat. He's the strangest fellow:

with a clutch of letters from Othello
such a mover and shaker in the bordello
and what a way with the violoncello!
so bello, so bello, so bello . . .
He waters the flowers with limoncello:

so mellow, so rose of Jericho, so Pirandello

The Lavender

was planted at the start.
It grew quickly, Napoleonic.
Battle manoeuvres at dawn, battle
manoeuvres at dusk. Strength
in numbers and such discipline.
Tunics shimmering in the breeze.

Sometimes we cut them back
and the stone terrace regains
its whiteness, the gecko hesitating –
Let's get the fuck out of here . . .

The cavalry retreats and gathers strength.
Thrum of bee, butterfly – and dragon flies
sent to check us out. They land on books,
shoulders, glasses, reconnaissance:
the lavender firing off volleys of sleep.

We wait like soldiers at Rourke's Drift,
wine bottles instead of rifles,
listening to the drum beat, the ululations.

Bee chant and cicada, butterflies as balletic
as Nureyev, all glitter and promiscuity.

Almost forty degrees.

We no longer have the strength or stomach
to fight the purple soldiers as they spread
across the terrace with their imperial blag.

Death by lavender. A slow death. Pray for us.

Oh readers, that was a long time ago.
Now we spread our insect wings and sob,
let the soldiers ride us in their hammocks.

Appetite, there's so much of it.

The Perfect Italian Subjunctive

was in the air
I could feel it coming in the air.

I was speaking to a gathering
of Italian Professors, grammarians,
philologists, beautiful people
who read Eugenio Montale for breakfast.

They could knock subjunctives around
all day like Gary Sobers.
They wore bow-ties and perfect trousers.
In fact the things they couldn't do
with a cuttlefish, the things they couldn't do!

I wanted a subjunctive in my mouth
so I opened it like a little bird
waiting for mother to drop one in.

Zombie Riviera

Quick! A last poem before I go / off my rocker

Frank O'Hara

The Italians are getting older.
That diet of theirs is a demographic killer.
They're pottering around on the edge of the cliff:
Che bello! the old people say, che bello!
They have no intention of leaping off.
They're going to live for another decade, at least.

They refuse to die.

The young have departed,
London mostly.

They've taken up work in
Tooting, Vauxhall and the City –

Gianni's working in a Sushi restaurant.

Leaving their mothers under the psychedelia of
bougainvillea and those long avenues of oleander.

There are no jobs on the Riviera.

Don't eat the oleander mother. It's poisonous.
Of course we won't carissimo, we'll eat more fish
and jangle our bangles.

The only young men in Liguria are Nigerians.
Strong, wiry, loquacious Nigerians.
They've been sent up from Lampedusa.
In Libya guns were pushed against their heads.
They were treated like slaves.

The world is not a kind place
but nevertheless the world is succulent.

Our people are dying
but the Italians on the Riviera live forever.

I'm English by the way, not Italian.
Oh, said Victor, I have an uncle in London.

I'm from Abuja. Greetings.
I am Victor from Abuja on the Italian Riviera.

Have you read Marinetti?
Fillipo Tomaso Marinetti –

Zang Tumb Tuuum

Italy is a land of the dead, a vast Pompeii,
white with sepulchres. We will destroy the museums,
the libraries, academies of every kind.

He didn't destroy the old people on the Riviera
because the old people are indestructible.

Zang Tumb Tuuum –

Where's mad Marinetti when you need him?
Dead –
Sometimes they pull Mussolini put of the grave,
put him on a balcony and shout Death or Glory.

It doesn't do much good.

The churches and the villas and the defunct kings
of Italy and the lachrymose marbled floors and
the chandeliers all crystallised in this everlasting grimace.

Sebastian the Golden Dog

Lorsica

Fiona and Gianmarco have gone to Sestri.
The valley is full of mist.
See you later, relax.
There's some cheese in the fridge
and a bowl of olives.
They've taken the dog, the golden dog.

Not a cigarette in the house, I've looked.
Not a cigarette in the valley.
Just a snowy owl turning its head.

They've taken Sebastian the golden dog
because they feared
I was going to turn him
into a Cuban cigar.

Long live Fidel Castro
and have a magnificent day!

Is that at all possible
in a village hanging
from the feet of Zeus

where Leonardo the Troubadour
has gone mad?

where Signora Volpone
has gone mad?

I'm going to found a university:
The University of Almost Anything

We believe in inanity
             banality
                     the cult of personality –

I am the Vice Chancellor and Acting Dean
Please make sure you've read
Beautiful Losers by week three.
There's going to be a symposium.

How cool is that?

Look, they've given me a Chair.
Even as I speak
I'm standing on it
and tying something round my neck
which feels suspiciously like rope.

Goodbye Blackbird

I had this ridiculous pang of nostalgia for Italian
bureaucracy so I got a cheap flight to Genoa and
then a taxi to the Municipal Hall in Corso Torino where,
with satisfaction, I joined a queue, a long queue.

I hadn't done this for twenty years but I recognised
several faces. I could see Serafina, somewhat older now.
Have you been here all this time? I asked. Oh Giulio, she said,
each time I get to the front they send me to the back,
it's like a game which never ends. *Un bel gioco dura poco*,
I said. How is the world outside? she asked. Have there been
any changes? Would you hold my hand a while?

Birth Certificates, Marriage Certificates, Residency
and Divorce Certificates and – along the corridor –
the nondescript Office of Death Certificates.

Should I get one now? Two pigeons with a single bean?
Are you dead already? asked the woman behind the screen.
You seem somewhat vertical for a corpse.
Not yet, I guess, I have a feeling that death's rather like a
blackbird. Really, she said, a blackbird, who would have thought!

I need a date and the cause of death – I'm not allowed to
leave it blank. That would be unconventional and probably
against the law. Well, you would be saving me time, or saving
someone else some time. In fact, you would be saving hours of time
which is a kindness in itself and I would never say a word to
anybody. Listen here, I have to sign it, and then stamp it with my
stamper. I see, the whole thing seems something of a nightmare,

                                    I said.

Blackbirds hey! However you are simpatico and actually
I remember you. Inglese non? Yes, signora, I am English.
My son works in London, she said, he lives in Tooting.
Tooting! Almost certainly a cause for celebration, I said.

I suppose another Death Certificate in the world
won't change much. Exactly, you choose the date and cause
of death and I won't look. Promise? she said. I promise. You write
in the details and it will be a secret I carry to the grave –
You sound like a nineteenth century novel! I do like Dickens,
she said, I even read *Bleak House* in English. I saw it as a kind
of penance, like a hundred Hail Marys and a great deal more
Pater Nosters. Now she was putting in the date and I looked away.

She smiled and took out her stamper and stamped it twice.
Grazie. Bella giornata, have a nice day, I said. And you too,
signor inglese. Let only beautiful things occur and keep
your eyes peeled. I waved to Serafina and stepped out
onto Corso Torino. The sun was shining, the birds
were singing and I walked to Bar Bliss and drank a Negroni.

Sopraelevata

We have taken the Sopraelevata, Eugenio hits
the accelerator, it's like a coronary bypass
through the city. We're driving past bedrooms,
cuttlefish, monuments, bridges –
Zena etherised on a post-industrial operating table:
Palazzo San Giorgio, Tower of Morchi, la Commenda di Pré
superannuated villas, the unforgiving labyrinth
Dino Campana psychotic in the back streets,
gin and tonic Don climbing into the pantheon
my young self weeping in some medieval doorway –
To the left of us the docks, the cranes, the sea
suppurating pullulating liners, oil tankers, refugees
and the light house, *la lanterna*, Ligurian tumescence.
We're driving through the gash of the city
unhealed wounds, the luxurious stigmata.
They beat the city black and blue and let it dangle on the cross.
My love, I think we're driving past a crucifixion!
Shipbuilders gone, chemical and steel plants gone
Cornigliano, old style sci-fi incinerator, closed –
spitting out gobs of toxicity. Ten minutes to reach the airport.
Non piangere! Non piangere!

Apollo and Marsyas

Poetry gigs would have
a certain style
if the poet deemed less successful
    got flayed alive.

The audience makes the decision –
who got the bigger cheer?
Didn't I? 'Fraid not mate. Sorry.

I reckon people would go to
poetry readings in larger numbers.

You'd have to think pretty carefully
before saying, Hello I've written
a poem about a lonely cow.

Forget Slams.

I can think of several people
who would flay the losing poet
with energy and glee.

Tenement Nights

You are my outer and my inner
my white-arsed sinner
my macaronic–macaroni dinner
my karaoke singer, that sudden glimmer
of quince trees and kumquat.
You are my west and east
Babette's Feast, the morning yeast
my north and south, my hole and mouth
my white fly, my chemical high
my overheated bliss, my Glasgow kiss
my bruises and excuses.
You are the passing ice cream van
the Zen gardens of Japan.
You are my transcendental spheres
those drooling éclairs.
You are my Cessnock, my Govan
my Ibrox, my Partick
you are my thistle, my thistle
my fine dining, my morning gristle.

Love

Those weeds on the tracks
in Bogliasco could be eaten
by a goat, should a goat
be arsed to clamber down the hill.

I want to call them yarrow
waiting quietly for the White Arrow –
yet they're purple, royal purple:

a little hoity for a weed
beloved of goats – daydreaming goats!

They are sovereign, growing
between the tracks, the drummer boys
of this quiet station.

Until the White Arrow hurtles through
and they swing to the left
or they swing to the right

as if they were being blasted
by an enormous hair dryer.

And when the train has shot past
they rattle furiously –
a kind of death-dance

or an act of flirtation:
as if to say to the goats on high
Come and eat us
lazy head-butting sweethearts

before we die.

Acknowledgements

Poems from *Heat Wave* have appeared in *Poetry Review, Spectator, The Honest Ulsterman, Ambit, Interpreter's House, Salamander* (USA), *Axon* (Australia), *The South Bank Magazine, The Dark Horse*, the *Vanguard* anthology edited by Richard Skinner (2019). 'The Crucible' won the Norwich Café Poets Comedic Prize, judged by Liz Berry. 'Toby's Singing' appeared in *Bollocks to Brexit: an Anthology of Poems and Short Fiction* (Civic Leicester, 2019, ed. Ambrose Misiyiwa). 'Eau Sauvage' was highly commended in the single poem Forward Prize and appears in the *Forward Book of Poetry* (2020). Similarly, 'Trolley Man' appears in the the *Forward Book of Poetry* (2021). Several poems appeared in *Average is the New Fantastico* (Green Bottle Press, 2019.)

There are many poet friends and colleagues who have provided encouragement in these challenging years. And thanks to Italian friends and the Bogliasco Foundation whose hospitality and kindness are a special gift. Massimo Bacigalupo, my Italian translator, has been a generous advocate for my poetry. *Grazie mille!* I'd like to thank Emily Berry whose sympathy for my writing and editorial rigour at the *Poetry Review* have been greatly appreciated.

Lightning Source UK Ltd.
Milton Keynes UK
UKHW012040280822
407942UK00001B/3